Life in Hot Places

Julie Haydon

Contents

Hot Places	2
Deserts	4
Desert Plants	5
Desert People	6
Desert Animals	8
Tropical Rainforests	10
Rainforest People	12
Rainforest Animals	14
Glossary	16

Hot Places

Some places on Earth get a lot of sunshine.

This place is very hot. It does not get much rain.

This hot place gets lots of rain.

Deserts

Deserts are very dry places. They do not get much rain.

Some deserts are made of sand. Some deserts have lots of rocks or stones.

Desert Plants

Desert plants can live in hot sunshine.

A cactus has water in its roots and **stem**.

Desert People

Some people live in deserts.

These desert people
live in tents.
They move from place
to place
to find food and water.

Some desert people dig holes
to get water
that is under the ground.

In some places,
water comes up
from under the ground.

Desert Animals

In the daytime,
lots of desert animals
stay under the ground,
or in the **shade**.
At night-time, they come out
to look for food to eat.

Some desert animals can live for a long time without water.

Tropical Rainforests

This is a tropical rainforest.
It is a hot place.
It gets lots of rain.

Tropical rainforests are full of plants.
The biggest trees get lots of sunshine.
Plants that grow under them do not get much sunshine.

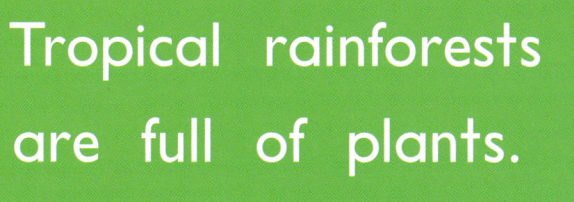

Rainforest People

Some people live in tropical rainforests. People live in this **village**.

They grow food in gardens and catch animals to eat.

Rainforest Animals

There are lots of good places for animals to live in a tropical rainforest. There is lots of food and water for animals, too.

This monkey lives in the trees of a tropical rainforest.
It eats leaves and fruit.

Glossary

shade

stem

village

16